Laurie Lee
Selected Poems

Unicorn, an imprint of Unicorn Publishing Group LLP
101 Wardour Street
London
W1F 0UG

www.unicornpublishing.org
www.laurielee.org

Published by Unicorn Press Ltd, 2014

ISBN 978-1-910065-14-3

10 9 8 7 6 5 4

Designed by Felicity Price-Smith
Printed in India by Imprint Press

Laurie Lee
Selected Poems

To Jessy

UNICORN

NOTE

Most of these verses were originally published in three separate volumes – spanning perhaps a decade or so – and for this selection I have cut them down by about half.

They were written by someone I once was and who is so distant to me now that I scarcely recognise him anymore. They speak for a time and a feeling which of course has gone from me, but for which I still have close affection and kinship.

L.L.

CONTENTS

INVASION SUMMER

The evening, the heather,
the unsecretive cuckoo
and butterflies in their disorder,
not a word of war as we lie
our mouths in a hot nest
and the flowers advancing.

Does a hill defend itself,
does a river run to earth
to hide its quaint neutrality?
A boy is shot with England in his brain,
but she lies brazen yet beneath the sun,
she has no honour and she has no fear.

A MOMENT OF WAR

It is night like a red rag
drawn across the eyes

the flesh is bitterly pinned
to desperate vigilance

the blood is stuttering with fear.

> *O praise the security of worms*
> *in cool crumbs of soil*
> *flatter the hidden sap*
> *and the lost unfertilized spawn of fish!*

The hands melt with weakness
into the gun's hot iron

the body melts with pity

the face is braced for wounds
the odour and the kiss of final pain.

> *O envy the peace of women*
> *giving birth and love like toys*
> *into the hands of men!*

The mouth chatters with pale curses

the bowels struggle like a nest of rats

the feet wish they were grass
spaced quietly.

>   *O Christ and Mother!*

But darkness opens like a knife for you
and you are marked down by your pulsing brain

and isolated

and your breathing,

your breathing is the blast, the bullet,
and the final sky.

Spanish frontier, 1937

WORDS ASLEEP

Now I am still and spent
and lie in a whited sepulchre
breathing dead

but there will be
no lifting of the damp swathes
no return of blood
no rolling away the stone

till the cocks carve sharp
gold scars in the morning
and carry the stirring sun
and early dust to my ears.

Andalucía

MUSIC IN A SPANISH TOWN

In the street I take my stand
with my fiddle like a gun against my shoulder,
and the hot strings under my trigger hand
shooting an old dance at the evening walls.

Each saltwhite house is a numbered tomb
each silent window crossed with blood;
my notes explode everywhere like bombs
when I should whisper in fear of the dead.

So my fingers falter, and run in the sun
like the limbs of a bird that is slain,
as my music searches the street in vain.

Suddenly there is a quick flutter of feet
and children crowd about me,
listening with sores and infected ears,
watching with lovely eyes and vacant lips.

Cordoba, 1936

JUNIPER

Juniper holds to the moon
a girl adoring a bracelet;
as the hills draw up their knees
they throw off their jasmine girdles.

You are a forest of game,
a thought of nights in procession,
you tread through the bitter fires
of the nasturtium.

I decorate you to a smell of apples,
I divide you among the voices
of owls and cavaliering cocks
and woodpigeons monotonously dry.

I hang lanterns on your mouth
and candles from your passionate crucifix,
and bloody leaves of the virginia
drip with their scarlet oil.

There is a pike in the lake
whose blue teeth eat the midnight stars
piercing the water's velvet skin
and puncturing your sleep.

I am the pike in your breast,
my eyes of clay revolve the waves
while cirrus roots and lilies grow
between our banks of steep embraces.

AT NIGHT

I think at night my hands are mad,
for they follow the irritant texture of darkness
continually carving the sad leaf of your mouth
in the thick black bark of sleep.

And my finger-joints are quick with insanity,
springing with lost amazement
through a vast waste of dreams
and forming frames of desire
around the thought of your eyes.

By day, the print of your body
is like a stroke of sun on my hands,
and the choir of your blood
goes chanting incessantly
through the echoing channels of my wrists.

But I am lost in my hut
when the stars are out,
for my palms have a catlike faculty of sight,
and the surface of every minute
is a swinging image of you.

LANDSCAPE

The season does not leave your limbs,
like a covered field you lie,
and remembering the exultant plough
your sheltered bosom stirs
and whispers warm with rain.

Waiting does not leave your eyes,
your belly is as bright as snow
and there your naked fingers
are spread over the dark flowers
shaking out their roots.

My kiss has not yet left your blood
but slumbers in a stream
within your quiet caves:
listening to the sun it will cry forth,
and burst with leaves, and blossom with a name.

THE ARMOURED VALLEY

Across the armoured valley trenched with light,
cuckoos pump forth their salvoes at the lark,
and blackbirds loud with nervous song and flight
shudder beneath the hawk's reconnaissance:
Spring is upon us, and our hopes are dark.

For as the petal and the painted cheek
issue their tactless beauties to the hour,
we must ignore the budding sun and seek
to camouflage compassion and ourselves
against the wretched icicles of war.

No festival of love will turn our bones
to flutes of frolic in this month of May,
but tools of hate shall make them into guns
and bore them for the piercing bullet's shout
and through their pipes drain all our blood away.

Yet though by sullen violence we are torn
from violet couches as the air grows sweet,
and by the brutal bugles of retreat
recalled to snows of death, yet Spring, repeat
your annual attack, pour through the breach
of some new heart your future victories.

LARCH TREE

Oh, larch tree with scarlet berries
sharpen the morning slender sun
sharpen the thin taste of September
with your aroma of sweet wax and powder delicate.

Fruit is falling in the valley
breaking on the snouts of foxes
breaking on the wooden crosses
where children bury the shattered bird.

Fruit is falling in the city
blowing a woman's eyes and fingers
across the street among the bones
of boys who could not speak their love.

I watch a starling cut the sky
a dagger through the blood of cold,
and grasses bound by strings of wind
stockade the sobbing fruit among the bees.

Oh, larch tree, with icy hair
your needles thread the thoughts of snow,
while in the fields a shivering girl
takes to her breasts the sad ripe apples.

THE THREE WINDS

The hard blue winds of March
shake the young sheep
and flake the long stone walls;
now from the gusty grass
comes the homed music of rams,
and plovers fall out of the sky
filling their wings with snow.

Tired of this northern tune
the winds turn soft
blowing white butterflies
out of the dog-rose hedges,
and schoolroom songs are full
of boys' green cuckoos
piping the summer round

Till August sends at last
its brick-red breath
over the baking wheat and blistered poppy,
brushing with feathered hands
the skies of brass,
with dreams of river moss
my thirst's delirium.

INTERVAL

All day the purple battle of love
as scented mouths position
soft fields of contesting langour
or jealous peaks of suspicion.

All day the trumpeting of fingers,
the endless march of desire
across the continent of an eyelid
or the desert of a hair.

How long we roam these territories
trailing our twin successes,
till the bending sun collapses
and I escape your kisses.

Then I drink the night like a coconut
and earth regains its shape;
at last the eunuch's neutral dream
and the beardless touch of sleep.

EQUINOX

Now tilts the sun his monument,
now sags his raw unwritten stone
deep in October's diamond clay.

And oozy sloes like flies are hung
malignant on the shrivelled stem,
too late to ripen, or to grow

Now is the time the wasp forsakes
the rose born like a weakly child
of earth-bed's pallor, death-bed's flush.

Time when the gourd upon the ground
cracks open kernel or decay
indifferent to man or worm.

Time of no violence, when at last
the shocked eye clears the battlefield
and burns down black the roots of grass.

And finds the prize of all its pain,
bedded in smoke, on leaves of blood -
love's charcoal cross, unlost, unwon.

MILKMAID

The girl's far treble, muted to the heat,
calls like a fainting bird across the fields
to where her flock lies panting for her voice,
their black horns buried deep in marigolds.

They climbed awake, like drowsy butterflies,
and press their red flanks through the tall branched grass,
and as they go their wandering tongues embrace
the vacant summer mirrored in their eyes.

Led to the limestone shadows of a barn
they snuff their past embalmèd in the hay,
while her cool hand, cupped to the udder's fount,
distils the brimming harvest of their day.

Look what a cloudy cream the earth gives out,
fat juice of buttercups and meadow-rye;
the girl dreams milk within her body's field
and hears, far off, her muted children cry.

VILLAGE OF WINTER CAROLS

Village of winter carols
and gawdy spinning tops,
of green-handed walnuts
and games in the moon.

You were adventure's web,
the flag of fear I flew
riding black stallions
through the rocky streets.

You were the first faint map
of the mysterious sun,
chart of my island flesh
and the mushroom-tasting kiss.

But no longer do I join
your children's sharp banditti,
nor seek the glamour of
your ravished apples.

Your hillocks build no more
their whales and pyramids,
nor howl across the night
their springing wolves.

For crouching in my brain
the crafty thigh of love
twists your old landscape
with a new device.

and every field has grown
a strange and flowering pit
where I must try the blind
and final trick of youth.

GUADALQUIVIR

Here on this desert plain
the fields are dust,
strangled by wind,
burnt by the quicklime sun.

But where the river's tongue
scoops out its channel deep
across the iron land
trees grow, and leaves
of vivid green
force back the baking air.

Fish and small birds
do strike with diamond mouths
the windows of the water,
while memories of song
and flowers flow
along the slender cables
of the mud.

So to the wires of love
do my limbs leap,
so does your finger draw
across my arid breast
torrents of melting snow
on threads of seed.

THE WILD TREES

O the wild trees of my home,
forests of blue dividing the pink moon,
the iron blue of those ancient branches
with their berries of vermilion stars.

In that place of steep meadows
the stacked sheaves are roasting,
and the sun-torn tulips
are tinders of scented ashes.

But here I have lost
the dialect of your hills,
my tongue has gone blind
far from their limestone roots.

Through trunks of black elder
runs a fox like a lantern,
and the hot grasses sing
with the slumber of larks.

But here there are thickets
of many different gestures,
torn branches of brick and steel
frozen against the sky.

O the wild trees of home
with their sounding dresses,
locks powdered with butterflies
and cheeks of blue moss.

I want to see you rise
from my brain's dry river,
I want your lips of wet roses
laid over my eyes.

O fountains of earth and rock,
gardens perfumed with cucumber,
home of secret valleys
where the wild trees grow.

Let me return at last
to your fertile wilderness
to sleep with the coiled fernleaves
in your heart's live stone.

CHRISTMAS LANDSCAPE

Tonight the wind gnaws
with teeth of glass,
the jackdaw shivers
in caged branches of iron,
the stars have talons.

There is hunger in the mouth
of vole and badger,
silver agonies of breath
in the nostril of the fox,
ice on the rabbit's paw.

Tonight has no moon,
no food for the pilgrim;
the fruit tree is bare,
the rose bush a thorn
and the ground bitter with stones.

But the mole sleeps, and the hedgehog
lies curled in a womb of leaves,
the bean and the wheat-seed
hug their germs in the earth
and the stream moves under the ice.

Tonight there is no moon,
but a new star opens
like a silver trumpet over the dead.
Tonight in a nest of ruins
the blessèd babe is laid.

And the fir tree warms to a bloom of candles,
the child lights his lantern,
stares at his tinselled toy;
our hearts and hearths
smoulder with live ashes.

In the blood of our grief
the cold earth is suckled,
in our agony the womb
convulses its seed,
in the last cry of anguish
the child's first breath is born.

POEM FOR EASTER

Wrapped in his shroud of wax, his swoon of wounds,
still as a winter's star he lies with death.

Still as a winter's lake his stark limbs lock
the pains that run in stabbing frosts around him.

Star in the lake, grey spark beneath the ice,
candle of love snuffed in its whitened flesh.

I, too, lie bound within your dawn of cold
while on my breath the serpent mortal moans.

O serpent in the egg, become a rod,
crack the stone shell that holds his light in coil.

O grief within the serpent sink your root
and bear the flower for which our forked tongues wail.

Cold in their hope our mortal eyes forgather,
wandering like moths about the tomb's shut mouth;

Waiting the word the riven rock shall utter,
waiting the dawn to fly its bird of god.

APRIL RISE

If ever I saw blessing in the air
    I see it now in this still early day
Where lemon-green the vaporous morning drips
    Wet sunlight on the powder of my eye.

Blown bubble-film of blue, the sky wraps round
    Weeds of warm light whose every root and rod
Splutters with soapy green, and all the world
    Sweats with the bead of summer in its bud.

If ever I heard blessing it is there
    Where birds in trees that shoals and shadows are
Splash with their hidden wings and drops of sound
    Break on my ears their crests of throbbing air.

Pure in the haze the emerald sun dilates,
    The lips of sparrows milk the mossy stones,
While white as water by the lake a girl
    Swims her green hand among the gathered swans.

Now, as the almond burns its smoking wick,
    Dropping small flames to light the candled grass;
Now, as my low blood scales its second chance,
    If ever world were blessèd, now it is.

FIRST LOVE

That was her beginning, an apparition
of rose in the unbreathed airs of his love,
her heart revealed by the wash of summer
sprung from her childhood's shallow stream.

Then it was that she put up her hair,
inscribed her eyes with a look of grief,
while her limbs grew as curious as coral branches,
her breast full of secrets.

But the boy, confused in his day's desire,
was searching for herons, his fingers bathed
in the green of walnuts, or watching at night
the Great Bear spin from the maypole star.

It was then that he paused in the death of a game,
felt the hook of her hair on his swimming throat,
saw her mouth at large in the dark river
flushed like a salmon.

But he covered his face and hid his joy
in a wild-goose web of false directions,
and hunted the woods for eggs and glow-worms,
for rabbits tasteless as moss.

And she walked in fields where the crocuses
branded her feet, and mares' tails sprang
from the prancing lake, and the salty grasses
surged round her stranded body.

THE LONG WAR

Less passionate the long war throws
its burning thorn about all men,
caught in one grief, we share one wound,
and cry one dialect of pain.

We have forgot who fired the house,
whose easy mischief spilt first blood,
under one raging roof we lie
the fault no longer understood.

But as our twisted arms embrace
the desert where our cities stood,
death's family likeness in each face
must show, at last, our brotherhood.

MOSS-ROSE

My mother would grow roses with each hand,
drawing them forth from country-frothing air.

Draw them, shape them, cut them from the thorn;
lay them like bleeding shells about the house.

And with my ears to the lips of those shell-roses
I harked to their humming seas, secret as hives.

And with my lips to those same rose-shell ears
I spoke my crimson words, my stinging brain.

With lips, ears, eyes, and every finger's nerve,
I moved, moth-throbbing, round each creviced fire.

As I do now, lost mother, country gone,
groping my grief around your moss-rose heart.

BIRD

O bird that was my vision,
my love, my dream that flew
over the famine-folded rocks,
the sky's reflected snow.

O bird that found and fashioned me,
that brought me from the land
safe in her singing cage of bone,
the webbed wings of her hand.

She took me to the topmost air,
curled in the atom of her eye,
and there I saw an island rise
out of the empty sea.

And falling there she set me down
naked on soil that knew no plough,
and loveless, speechless, I beheld
the world's beginning grow.

And there I slew her for my bread
and in her feathers dressed;
and there I raised a paradise
from the seed in her dead breast.

BLACK EDGE

I lie no more in a healthy sheet,
a wind of chill eyes makes a marsh of my cheeks,
diseased is my sleep with demented sound
    and I am infected by the stars.

For see how the sun rubs ulcers in the sky,
how black as bats the field flowers droop and fall;
    the earth, the sweet earth
    is foul and full of graves.

O save me, for I am sick:
lay on my eyelids your finger's miracle,
    bewitch me that I may live.

Wash me in happy air,
restore me with the odour of rivers;
    then feed, O feed
    my sight with your normal love.

THISTLE

Thistle, blue bunch of daggers
rattling upon the wind,
saw-tooth that separates
the lips of grasses.

Your wound in childhood was
a savage shock of joy
that set the bees on fire
and the loud larks singing.

Your head enchanted then
smouldering among the flowers
filled the whole sky with smoke
and sparks of seed.

Now from your stabbing bloom's
nostalgic point of pain
ghosts of those summers rise
rustling across my eyes.

Seeding a magic thorn
to prick the memory,
to start in my icy flesh
fevers of long lost fields.

MY MANY-COATED MAN

Under the scarlet-licking leaves,
through bloody thought and bubbly shade,
the padded, spicy tiger moves –
a sheath of swords, a hooded blade.

The turtle on the naked sand
peels to the air his pewter snout
and rubs the sky with slotted shell –
the heart's dismay turned inside out.

The rank red fox goes forth at night
to bite the gosling's downy throat,
then digs his grave with panic claws
to share oblivion with the stoat.

The mottled moth, pinned to a tree,
woos with his wings the bark's disease
and strikes a fungoid, fevered pose
to live forgotten and at ease.

Like these, my many-coated man
shields his hot hunger from the wind,
and, hooded by a smile, commits
his private murder in the mind.

SUMMER RAIN

Where in the valley the summer rain
Moves crazed and chill through the crooked trees
The briars bleed green, and the far fox-banks
Their sharp cries tangle in sobbing shades.

I hear the sad rinsing of reeded meadows
The small lakes rise in the wild white rose
The shudder of wings in the streaming cedars
And tears of lime running down from the hills.

All day in the tomb of my brain I hear
The cold wheat whisper, the veiled trees mourn,
And behold through windows of weighted ivy
The wet walls blossom with silver snails.

The heron flies up from the stinging waters,
The white swan droops by the dripping reed,
And summer lies swathed in its ripeness, exuding
Damp odours of lilies and alabaster.

In a fever of June she is wrapped and anointed
With deathly sweating of cold jasmine,
And her petals weep wax to the thick green sky
Like churchyard wreaths under domes of glass.

Too long hangs the light in the valley lamenting,
The slow rain sucking the sun's green eye;
And too long do you hide in your vault of clay
While I search for your passion's obliterate stone.

Let the dark night come, let it crack of doom
The sky's heart shatter and empty grief,
The storm fetch its thunder of hammers and axes,
The green hills break as our graves embrace.

FIELD OF AUTUMN

Slow moves the acid breath of noon
over the copper-coated hill,
slow from the wild crab's bearded breast
the palsied apples fall.

Like coloured smoke the day hangs fire,
taking the village without sound;
the vulture-headed sun lies low
chained to the violet ground.

The horse upon the rocky height
rolls all the valley in his eye,
but dares not raise his foot or move
his shoulder from the fly.

The sheep, snail-backed against the wall.
lifts her blind face but does not know
the cry her blackened tongue gives forth
is the first bleat of snow.

Each bird and stone, each roof and well,
feels the gold foot of autumn pass;
each spider binds with glittering snare
the splintered bones of grass.

Slow moves the hour that sucks our life,
slow drops the late wasp from the pear,
the rose tree's thread of scent draws thin -
and snaps upon the air.

DAY OF THESE DAYS

Such a morning it is when love
leans through geranium windows
and calls with a cockerel's tongue.

When red-haired girls scamper like roses
over the rain-green grass,
and the sun drips honey.

When hedgerows grow venerable,
berries dry black as blood,
and holes suck in their bees.

Such a morning it is when mice
run whispering from the church,
dragging dropped ears of harvest.

When the partridge draws back his spring
and shoots like a buzzing arrow
over grained and mahogany fields.

When no table is bare,
and no breast dry,
and the tramp feeds off ribs of rabbit.

Such a day it is when time
piles up the hills like pumpkins,
and the streams run golden.

When all men smell good,
and the cheeks of girls
are as baked bread to the mouth.

As bread and bean flowers
the touch of their lips
and their white teeth sweeter than cucumbers.

BOY IN ICE

O river, green and still,
By frost and memory stayed,
Your dumb and stiffened glass divides
A shadow and a shade.

In air, the shadow's face
My winter gaze lets fall
To see beneath the stream's bright bars
That other shade in thrall.

A boy, time-fixed in ice,
His cheeks with summer dyed,
His mouth, a rose-devouring rose,
His bird-throat petrified.

O fabulous and lost,
More distant to me now
Than rock-drawn mammoth, painted stag
Or tigers in the snow.

You stare into my face
Dead as ten thousand years,
Your sparrow tongue sealed in my mouth
Your world about my ears.

And till our shadows meet,
Till time burns through the ice,
Thus frozen shall we ever stay
Locked in this paradise.

THE EDGE OF DAY

The dawn's precise pronouncement waits
With breath of light indrawn,
Then forms with smoky, smut-red lips
The great O of the sun.

The mouldering atoms of the dark
Blaze into morning air;
The birdlike stars droop down and die,
The starlike birds catch fire.

The thrush's tinder throat strikes up,
The sparrow chips hot sparks
From flinty tongue, and all the sky
Showers with electric larks.

And my huge eye a chaos is
Where molten worlds are born;
Where floats the eagle's flaming moon,
And crows, like clinkers, burn;

Where blackbirds scream with comet tails,
And flaring finches fall,
And starlings, aimed like meteors,
Bounce from the garden wall;

Where, from the edge of day I spring
Alive for mortal flight,
Lit by the heart's exploding sun
Bursting from night to night.

TWELFTH NIGHT

No night could be darker than this night,
no cold so cold,
as the blood snaps like a wire,
and the heart's sap stills,
and the year seems defeated.

O never again, it seems, can green things run,
or sky birds fly,
or the grass exhale its humming breath
powdered with pimpernels,
from this dark lung of winter.

Yet here are lessons for the final mile
of pilgrim kings;
the mile still left when all have reached
their tether's end: that mile
where the Child lies hid.

For see, beneath the hand, the earth already
warms and glows;
for men with shepherd's eyes there are
signs in the dark, the turning stars,
the lamb's returning time.

Out of this utter death he's born again,
his birth our saviour;
from terror's equinox he climbs and grows,
drawing his finger's light across our blood -
the sun of heaven, and the son of god.

THE EASTER GREEN

Not dross, but dressed with good,
Is this gold air;
Not bald nor bare
But bearded like a god
Grown old more fair.

Dazed from the pit I see
Glazes of holy light
On day and diamond night;
Through every sun I hear
The chiming aconite.

By husk and darkness fed
My appetite grows keen,
By buried lusts made lean
Child-tongued I suck sweet bread
And kiss the virgin green.

I, from the well new-drawn,
With root and flower am crowned -
Drowsed, but not drowned.
The Easter-father blesses with a lamb;
The son is not disowned.

So shall I know, come fall,
Come flesh returning frail,
This shriving shall not fail:
The green blood flushing at the heart
Anoints the prodigal.

SUNKEN EVENING

The green light floods the city square –
A sea of fowl and feathered fish,
Where squalls of rainbirds dive and splash
And gusty sparrows chop the air.

Submerged, the prawn-blue pigeons feed
In sandy grottoes round the Mall,
And crusted lobster-buses crawl
Among the fountain's silver weed.

There, like a wreck, with mast and bell,
The torn church settles by the bow,
While phosphorescent starlings stow
Their mussel shells along the hull.

The oyster-poet, drowned but dry,
Rolls a black pearl between his bones;
The typist, trapped by telephones,
Gazes in bubbles at the sky.

Till, with the dark, the shallows run,
And homeward surges tide and fret –
The slow night trawls its heavy net
And hauls the clerk to Surbiton.

THE POLLARD BEECH

Blue-pencil knife, to keep it brief,
Edits the sprawled loquacious beech,
And clips each hyperbolic leaf
To fit the city's stumpy speech.

Till, like a slogan, trim and terse,
It stands and sums up in a word
The gist of that once epic verse
Whose every branch rhymed with a bird.

SONG BY THE SEA

Girl of green waters, liquid as lies,
Cool as the calloused snow,
From my attic brain and prisoned eyes
Draw me and drown me now.

O suck me down to your weeds and fates,
Green horizontal girl,
And in your salt-bright body breed
My death's dream-centred pearl.

For locked alive in the brutal bone
I feel my lust of love
Rolling her porpoise thighs alone
Where the tropic channels move.

Her smooth mouth moons among the tides
Sipping the milky fishes,
Her fallow, shallow breasts pile up
Tight with my secret wishes.

Girl of green waters, liquid as light,
Beneath your skin of suns
My frights and frenzies moan asleep,
My deeds are skeletons.

So suck me down to your bed of sand,
Dilute my serpent blood,
Then lift the stain from my crimson hand
And sink it in your flood.

LONG SUMMER

Gold as an infant's humming dream,
Stamped with its timeless, tropic blush,
The steady sun stands in the air
And burns like Moses' holy bush.

And burns while nothing it consumes;
The smoking branch but greener grows,
The crackling briar, from budded lips,
A floating stream of blossom blows.

A daze of hours, a blaze of noons,
Licks my cold shadow from the ground;
A flaming trident rears each dawn
To stir the blood of earth around.

Unsinged beneath the furnace sky
The frenzied beetle runs reborn,
The ant his antic mountain moves,
The rampant ram rewinds his horn.

I see the crazy bees drop fat
From tulips ten times gorged and dry;
I see the sated swallow plunge
To drink the dazzled waterfly.

A halo flares around my head,
A sunflower flares across the sun,
While down the summer's seamless haze
Such feasts of milk and honey run

That lying with my orchid love,
Whose kiss no frost of age can sever,
I cannot doubt the cold is dead,
The gold earth turned to good – forever.

SCOT IN THE DESERT

All day the sand, like golden chains,
The desert distance binds;
All day the crouching camels groan,
Whipped by the gritty winds.

The mountain, flayed by sun, reveals
Red muscles, wounds of stone,
While on its face the black goats swarm
And bite it to the bone.

Here light is death; on every rock
It stretches like a cry,
Its fever burns up every bush,
It drinks each river dry.

It cracks with thirst the creviced lip,
It fattens black the tongue,
It turns the storm cloud into dust,
The morning dew to dung.

Men were not made to flourish here,
They shroud their heads and fly -
Save one, who stares into the sun
With sky-blue British eye.

Who stares into the zenith sun
And smiles and feels no pain,
Blood-cooled by Calvin, mist and bog,
And summers in the rain.

TO MATTHEW SMITH

Fused with the minerals of sun and earth,
spurting with smoke of flowers,
oil is incendiary on your moving brush;
your hands are jets
that crack the landscape's clinker and draw forth
its buried incandescence.

These molten moments brazed in field and flesh
burn out for us,
but you can stand and nail within a frame
the fire we mourn,
can catch the pitchpine hour and keep its flame
pinned at the point of heat.

Our summer's noon you pour into a mould,
a rose its furnace;
through green and blue its burning seeds unfold,
through night and day:
raked by your eyes the paint has never cooled.

COCK-PHEASANT

Gilded with leaf-thick paint; a steady
Eye fixed like a ruby rock;
Across the cidrous banks of autumn
Swaggers the stamping pheasant-cock.

The thrusting nut and bursting apple
Accompany his jointed walk,
The creviced pumpkin and the marrow
Bend to his path on melting stalk.

Sure as an Inca priest or devil,
Feathers stroking down the corn,
He blinks the lively dust of daylight,
Blind to the hunter's powder-horn.

For me, alike, this flushed October –
Ripe, and round-fleshed, and bellyfull –
Fevers me fast but cannot fright, though
Each dropped leaf shows the winter's skull.

TOWN OWL

On eves of cold, when slow coal fires,
rooted in basements, burn and branch,
brushing with smoke the city air;

When quartered moons pale in the sky,
and neons glow along the dark
like deadly nightshade on a briar;

Above the muffled traffic then
I hear the owl, and at his note
I shudder in my private chair.

For like an augur he has come
to roost among our crumbling walls,
his blooded talons sheathed in fur.

Some secret lure of time it seems
has called him from his country wastes
to hunt a newer wasteland here.

And where the candelabra swung,
bright with the dancers' thousand eyes,
now his black, hooded pupils stare.

And where the silk-shoed lovers ran
with dust of diamonds in their hair,
he opens now his silent wing,

And, like a stroke of doom, drops down,
and swoops across the empty hall,
and plucks a quick mouse off the stair...

HOME FROM ABROAD

Far-fetched with tales of other worlds and ways,
My skin well-oiled with wines of the Levant,
I set my face into a filial smile
To greet the pale, domestic kiss of Kent.

But shall I never learn? That gawky girl,
Recalled so primly in my foreign thoughts,
Becomes again the green-haired queen of love
Whose wanton form dilates as it delights.

Her rolling tidal landscape floods the eye
And drowns Chianti in a dusky stream;
The flower-flecked grasses swim with simple horses,
The hedges choke with roses fat as cream.

So do I breathe the hayblown airs of home,
And watch the sea-green elms drip birds and shadows,
And as the twilight nets the plunging sun
My heart's keel slides to rest among the meadows.

APPLES

Behold the apples' rounded worlds:
juice-green of July rain,
the black polestar of flowers, the rind
mapped with its crimson stain.

The russet, crab and cottage red
burn to the sun's hot brass,
then drop like sweat from every branch
and bubble in the grass.

They lie as wanton as they fall,
and where they fall and break,
the stallion clamps his crunching jaws,
the starling stabs his beak.

In each plump gourd the cidery bite
of boys' teeth tears the skin;
the waltzing wasp consumes his share,
the bent worm enters in.

I, with as easy hunger, take
entire my season's dole;
welcome the ripe, the sweet, the sour,
the hollow and the whole.

THE ABANDONED SHADE

Walking the abandoned shade
of childhood's habitations,
my ears remembering chime,
hearing their buried voices.

Hearing original summer,
the birdlit banks of dawn,
the yellow-hammer beat of blood
gilding my cradle eyes.

Hearing the tin-moon rise
and the sunset's penny fall,
the creep of frost and weep of thaw
and bells of winter robins.

Hearing again the talking house
and the four vowels of the wind,
and midnight monsters whispering
in the white throat of my room.

Season and landscape's liturgy,
badger and sneeze of rain,
the bleat of bats, and bounce of rabbits
bubbling under the hill:

Each old and echo-salted tongue
sings to my backward glance;
but the voice of the boy, the boy I seek,
within my mouth is dumb.

BOMBAY ARRIVAL

Slow-hooved across the carrion sea,
Smeared by the betel-spitting sun,
Like cows the Bombay islands come
Dragging the mainland into view.

The loose flank loops the rocky bone,
The light beats thin on horn and hill;
Still breeds the flesh for hawks, and still
The Hindu heart drips on a stone.

Around the wide dawn-ridden bay
The waters move their daggered wings;
The dhow upon its shadow clings –
A dark moth pinioned to the day.

False in the morning, screened with silk,
Neat as an egg the Town draws near,
False as a map her streets appear
Ambling, and odourless as milk.

Until she holds us face to face –
A crumbling mask with bullet pores,
A nakedness of jewels and sores
Clutched with our guilt in her embrace.

ON BEACON HILL

Now as we lie beneath the sky,
Prone and knotted, you and I,
Visible at last we are
To each nebula and star.

Here as we kiss, the bloodless moon
Stirs to our rustling breath; Saturn
Leans us a heavy-lidded glance
And knows us for his revenants.

Arching, our bodies gather light
From suns long lost to human sight,
Our lips contain a dust of heat
Drawn from the burnt-out infinite.

The speechless conflict of our hands
Ruffles the red Mars' desert sands
While coupled in our doubled eyes
Jupiter dishevelled lies.

Now as we loose the knots of love,
Earth at our back and sky above,
Visible at last we gather
All that is, except each other.

SHOT FOX

He lay in April
like a shaft of autumn
reddening the leaves,
his tail a brush-fire or
a meteor burning
the white-starred wood.

Choked he had fallen
in mid-thrust of air,
taking the brittle asteroids across his shoulders
– space-hot, a leaden shower –
cutting him down.

Stark as a painted board
the checked limbs wrote
his leaping epitaph,
where he, all power, had made
his last free race –
stopped by the gun.

Now stretched, an arc of fur,
death drinks his lungs,
and in his eyes,
arrowed towards his den,
a blunted light…

The child first found him –
dropping her hot-held flowers
for better things;
fell on one knee and stroked
his bitter teeth,
glad of her luck.

GIRL UNDER FIG-TREE

Slim girl, slow burning
quick to run
under the fig-tree's
loaded fruits.

Skin-cold like them
your wet teeth spread,
parting pink
effervescent lips.

When I hold you here
valleys of fruit and flesh
bind me
now wet, now dry.

While on your eyes, the cool
green-shaded lids
close on the
wells of summer.

Slim girl, slow burning
quick to rise
between question
and loaded promise.

If I take you, peel you
against the noonday dark,
blind wasps
drill my hands like stars.

NIGHT SPEECH
(for a Shakespeare Festival)

The bright day is done
and we are for the dark;

but not for death.

We are, as eyelids fall
and night's silk rises,
stalled in our sleep
to watch the written dark,
brighter than day,
rephrase our stuttered past.

This fur-lined hour
makes princes of each wretch
whose day-bed wasted,
points each lax tongue
to daggered brightness,
says what we could not say.

Awake, we stumbled; now
dream-darting truth
homes to each flying wish;
and love replays its hand,
aims its dark pinions nobly,
even its treacheries…

Night, that renews, re-orders
day's scattered dust,
shake now from sleep's long lips
all we have lost and done,
stars, pearls and leaded tears
on our closed eyes;

and we are for the dark

STORK IN JEREZ

White arched, in loops of silence, the bodega
Lies drowsed in spices, where the antique woods,
Piled in solera, dripping years of flavour,
Distil their golden fumes among the shades.

In from the yard - where barrels under figtrees
Split staves of sunlight from the noon's hot glare –
The tall stork comes; black-stilted, sagely-witted,
Wiping his careful beak upon the air.

He is a priestlike presence, he inscribes
Sharp as a pen his staid and written dance,
Skating the floor with stiffened plumes behind him,
Gravely off-balance, solemn in his trance.

Drunk on these sherry vapours, eyes akimbo,
He treads among the casks, makes a small leap,
Flaps wildly, fails to fly – until at last,
Folded umbrella-wise, he falls asleep.

So bird and bard exchange their spheres of pleasure:
He, from his high-roofed nest now levelled lies;
Whilst I, earth-tied, breathing these wines take wing
And float amazed across his feathered skies.

FISH AND WATER

A golden fish like a pint of wine
Rolls the sea undergreen,
Glassily balanced on the tide
Only the skin between.

Fish and the water lean together,
Separate and one,
Till a fatal flash of the instant sun
Lazily corkscrews down.

Did fish and water drink each other?
The reed leans there alone;
As we, who once drank each other's breath,
Have emptied the air, and gone.

SEAFRONT

Here like the maze of our bewilderment
the thorn-crowned wire spreads high along the shore,
and flowers with rust, and tears our common sun;
and where no paths of love may reach the sea
the shut sands wait deserted for the drowned.

On other islands similarly barbed
mankind lies self-imprisoned in his fear,
and watches through the black sights of a gun
the winging flocks of migratory birds
who cannot speak of freedom, yet are free.